I0477652

UNPLUGGED REDISCOVERING JOY IN A DIGITAL-FREE LIFE

A guide to taking breaks from technology, reducing screen time, and finding fulfillment through offline activities and real-world interactions

By

Benjamin Grace.

TABLE OF CONTENTS

INTRODUCTION

In today's fast-paced, hyper-connected world, our lives are dominated by screens. From the moment we wake up to the time we go to bed, we are tethered to our smartphones, tablets, computers, and televisions. We check emails, scroll through social media, binge-watch our favorite shows, and constantly stay updated with the latest news. While technology has undoubtedly brought convenience and innovation to our lives, it has also created a relentless demand for our attention, often leaving us feeling overwhelmed, stressed, and disconnected from the real world.

Welcome to Unplugged Rediscovering Joy in a Digital-Free Life.

This book is your guide to taking a step back from the digital noise and reconnecting with what truly matters. It's about finding balance in an increasingly digital world, reducing screen time, and discovering fulfillment through offline activities and real-world interactions. Whether you're looking to improve your mental clarity, strengthen your relationships, or simply find more joy in everyday life, this book is here to help you navigate the path toward a healthier, more intentional way of living.

Why Unplug?

The idea of unplugging from our digital devices can seem daunting, even unimaginable for some. But the benefits of reducing screen time are profound and far-reaching. Studies have shown that excessive screen time can lead to various physical and mental health issues, including eye strain, sleep disturbances, anxiety, and depression. More importantly, our constant attachment to screens often comes at the expense of our real-world relationships and experiences. We miss out on the beauty of a sunset, the joy of a meaningful conversation, or the simple pleasure of reading a book.

What You'll Discover in This Book

Chapter 1: The Ubiquity of Screens - We begin with a deep dive into how screens dominate our daily lives and the science behind the effects of prolonged screen exposure on our health. Understanding the extent of our digital dependence is the first step toward making meaningful changes.

Chapter 2: The Benefits of Unplugging- Here, we explore the myriad benefits of reducing screen time, from improved mental clarity and focus to enhanced emotional well-being and stronger relationships. Unplugging isn't just about cutting back on technology; it's about enriching your life in countless ways.

Chapter 3: Creating a Digital Detox Plan - This chapter provides practical steps to help you create a personalized digital detox plan. You'll learn how to set intentions, assess your current usage, and establish healthy boundaries to minimize screen time effectively.

Chapter 4: Embracing Offline Activities- Discover the joy of rediscovering old hobbies and finding new ones that don't involve screens. Whether it's picking up a musical instrument, diving into a good book, or exploring new creative outlets, this chapter is filled with inspiration for screen-free activities.

Chapter 5: Reconnecting with Nature - We delve into the healing power of nature and how spending time outdoors can rejuvenate your mind and body. From simple gardening to adventurous hikes, you'll find practical tips to incorporate nature into your daily routine.

Chapter 6: Enhancing Real-World Connections - Learn strategies for building stronger relationships through improved communication, community engagement, and screen-free socializing. Real-world connections are essential for a fulfilling life, and this chapter shows you how to nurture them.

Chapter 7: Digital Minimalism - Embrace the principles of digital minimalism to simplify your life and maintain a balanced approach to technology use. This chapter offers practical tips for decluttering your digital space and adopting sustainable digital practices.

Chapter 8: Navigating Work and Technology - Striking a balance between work and life in a digital world can be challenging. Discover strategies for maintaining a healthy work-life balance, staying productive without constant screen use, and creating tech-free workspaces.

Chapter 9: Mindful Technology Use - Mindfulness isn't just for meditation; it's a powerful tool for intentional technology use. Learn techniques for conscious consumption, mindful usage habits, and the benefits of digital detox retreats.

Chapter 10: Long-Term Success - Finally, we'll discuss strategies for maintaining momentum, celebrating progress, and inspiring others to join you on this journey. Embracing a balanced life is an ongoing process, and this chapter helps you stay motivated for the long term.

A Journey Worth Taking

Unplugging and rediscovering joy in a digital-free life is a journey worth taking. It's about reclaiming your time, nurturing your well-being, and finding deeper connections with the world around you. This book is not about completely abandoning technology; rather, it's about using it mindfully and intentionally, ensuring it serves you rather than controls you.

As you embark on this journey, remember that every small step counts. The goal is not perfection but progress. By taking the time to unplug, even if only for a few minutes each day, you'll start to notice significant improvements in your mental clarity, emotional health, and overall quality of life.

Thank you for choosing to read this book. Together, let's rediscover the joy and fulfillment that comes from living a balanced, intentional, and digitally mindful life. Let's get started on this transformative journey to a more connected and joyful existence beyond the screens.

CHAPTER 1

UNDERSTANDING THE DIGITAL OVERLOAD

THE UBIQUITY OF SCREENS

In today's world, screens are everywhere. From the moment we wake up to the time we go to bed, our eyes are glued to various screens—smartphones, tablets, computers, TVs, and even smartwatches. It's astonishing how integral these devices have become to our daily routines. Think about it: how often do you check your phone first thing in the morning or use your computer at work? The average person spends about 11 hours a day interacting with screens. This chapter explores how deeply embedded screens are in every aspect of our lives and how they shape our daily experiences.

Screens have revolutionized the way we work, communicate, and entertain ourselves. Emails, video calls, social media, streaming services, online shopping—the list is endless. While these advancements have made our lives more convenient, they've also created a constant demand for our attention. We live in a state of perpetual connectivity, where notifications and updates keep us tethered to our devices. This constant engagement can lead to a sense of overload and overwhelm, as our brains struggle to process the sheer volume of information bombarding us daily.

But it's not just about the quantity of screen time; it's also about the quality. How are we spending those hours in front of screens? Are we engaging in meaningful activities, or are we mindlessly scrolling through social media feeds? This chapter will delve into these questions, encouraging you to reflect on your screen habits and how they align with your values and priorities.

THE SCIENCE OF SCREEN TIME

The effects of prolonged screen exposure on our mental and physical health are profound and far-reaching. Let's dive into some of the key findings from scientific research to understand how screens impact us:

MENTAL HEALTH:Numerous studies have shown a correlation between excessive screen time and mental health issues such as anxiety, depression, and stress. Social media, in particular, can contribute to feelings of inadequacy and loneliness as we compare our lives to the curated, often idealized images and stories shared by others. The constant barrage of information and notifications can also lead to cognitive overload, making it difficult to concentrate and process information effectively.

SLEEP DISRUPTION: Blue light emitted by screens interferes with the production of melatonin, the hormone responsible for regulating sleep. This disruption can lead to difficulties falling asleep and staying asleep, resulting in poor sleep quality. Inadequate sleep, in turn, affects our mood, energy levels, and overall well-being.

PHYSICAL HEALTH: Prolonged screen time is associated with a sedentary lifestyle, which increases the risk of obesity, cardiovascular disease, and other health problems. Additionally, staring at screens for long periods can cause eye strain, headaches, and neck and shoulder pain—a condition often referred to as "tech neck."

Understanding these impacts is crucial for making informed decisions about our screen use. By recognizing the potential risks, we can take proactive steps to mitigate them and prioritize our health and well-being.

RECOGNIZING DIGITAL DEPENDENCE

Digital dependence is more common than we might think. But how do we know if we're becoming overly reliant on our screens? Here are some signs to watch for:

CONSTANT CHECKING:Do you find yourself reaching for your phone first thing in the morning and frequently throughout the day? Do you feel anxious or irritable when you can't check your messages or notifications?

DIFFICULTY DISCONNECTING:Are you unable to put your phone away during meals, conversations, or other activities? Do you feel compelled to check your devices even when you're supposed to be relaxing or spending time with loved ones?

IMPACT ON RELATIONSHIPS: Is your screen time interfering with your relationships? Are you more focused on your device than on the people around you? Do you find it challenging to have meaningful, face-to-face conversations without the distraction of screens?

NEGLECTING RESPONSIBILITIES:Is your screen use affecting your productivity at work or school? Are you neglecting household chores, hobbies, or self-care activities because you're spending too much time online?

Recognizing these signs is the first step toward addressing digital dependence. It's important to approach this topic with compassion and understanding, acknowledging that screens are designed to be engaging and that breaking free from digital habits can be challenging. However, by becoming aware of our screen use patterns and their impact on our lives, we can begin to make conscious choices that support our well-being and help us rediscover the joy of a more balanced, digital-free life.

In this chapter, we've explored how screens dominate our daily lives, the scientific impacts of prolonged screen exposure, and the signs of digital dependence. As we move forward, we'll delve into practical strategies for reducing screen time and finding fulfillment through offline activities. So, let's take the first step toward reclaiming our time and rediscovering the joy of a more present, engaged life.

CHAPTER 2

THE BENEFITS OF UNPLUGGING

MENTAL CLARITY AND FOCUS

Imagine starting your day without the immediate distraction of notifications, emails, and social media updates. By reducing screen time, you give your brain a chance to rest and recharge, leading to improved mental clarity and focus. Here's how unplugging can benefit your cognitive function:

ENHANCED CONCENTRATION: Constant notifications and the urge to check our devices create a fragmented attention span. By taking breaks from screens, you can regain the ability to concentrate on tasks for longer periods. This means you can work more efficiently and effectively, producing higher-quality results in less time.

IMPROVED MEMORY: Excessive screen time, especially involving multitasking, can impair memory and cognitive function. When you unplug, your brain has more space to process and store information, leading to better recall and retention of important details.

INCREASED CREATIVITY:Stepping away from screens allows your mind to wander and daydream, which is crucial for creative thinking. Engaging in offline activities like reading, drawing, or spending time in nature can stimulate your imagination and lead to innovative ideas and solutions.

REDUCED COGNITIVE OVERLOAD: Our brains are not designed to handle the constant influx of information that screens provide. This cognitive overload can lead to mental fatigue and burnout. Unplugging gives your mind a much-needed break, helping you feel more refreshed and ready to tackle challenges with a clear head.

By consciously reducing screen time, you create an environment where your brain can thrive, leading to sharper focus, better memory, and increased creativity. These benefits not only enhance your productivity but also contribute to a greater sense of mental well-being.

EMOTIONAL WELL-BEING
Our emotional health is closely tied to our screen habits. Let's explore the profound impact that unplugging can have on your mood, anxiety levels, and overall emotional well-being:

IMPROVED MOOD: Excessive screen time, particularly on social media, can lead to negative comparisons, feelings of inadequacy, and even depression. By limiting your exposure to these platforms, you can protect yourself from the constant barrage of unrealistic portrayals and negative news. Instead, you'll have more time to engage in activities that genuinely bring you joy and fulfillment.

REDUCED ANXIETY:The pressure to stay connected and constantly respond to messages and notifications can create a sense of urgency and anxiety. Unplugging allows you to slow down and be present in the moment, reducing stress and promoting a calmer state of mind. Practices like mindfulness and meditation become more accessible when you're not constantly distracted by screens.

BETTER SLEEP:Blue light emitted by screens interferes with the production of melatonin, the hormone responsible for regulating sleep. By reducing screen time, especially before bed, you can improve your sleep quality. A good night's sleep is essential for emotional stability, as it helps regulate mood and stress levels.

INCREASED SELF-ESTEEM: Taking breaks from social media and other screen-based activities allows you to reconnect with your true self, free from external validation. Engaging in offline activities that you enjoy and excel at can boost your self-esteem and foster a healthier self-image.

By prioritizing your emotional well-being and reducing screen time, you'll find that you feel happier, more relaxed, and better equipped to handle life's challenges. This positive shift in your emotional state can have a ripple effect, enhancing all areas of your life.

STRENGTHENING RELATIONSHIPS
One of the most rewarding benefits of unplugging is the opportunity to strengthen your relationships with loved ones. Let's explore how reducing screen time can lead to deeper, more meaningful connections:

QUALITY TIME:When you're not constantly distracted by screens, you can fully engage in the present moment with the people around you. Whether it's sharing a meal, having a heartfelt conversation, or enjoying a fun activity together, quality time spent without screens fosters stronger bonds and deeper connections.

BETTER COMMUNICATION:Face-to-face interactions are essential for building trust and understanding in relationships. Without the barrier of screens, you can communicate more effectively, picking up on non-verbal cues like body language and facial expressions. This leads to more genuine and meaningful exchanges.

SHARED EXPERIENCES:Unplugging allows you to create and share experiences with your loved ones. Whether it's going for a hike, playing a board game, or simply sitting together and talking, these shared moments create lasting memories and reinforce your connection.

MODELING HEALTHY HABITS: By consciously reducing your screen time, you set a positive example for those around you, especially children. Demonstrating the importance of real-world interactions and offline activities can encourage others to adopt similar habits, leading to a more connected and fulfilling family and social life.

Strengthening your relationships through unplugging not only enriches your own life but also positively impacts those around you. The joy and fulfillment that come from deep, meaningful connections are irreplaceable and can lead to a happier, more balanced life.

Exploring the benefits of unplugging—from improved mental clarity and emotional well-being to stronger relationships—you can see how taking intentional breaks from screens can transform your life. Each of these benefits contributes to a richer, more joyful existence, helping you rediscover the beauty and fulfillment of a digital-free life. So, let's embrace the power of unplugging and start experiencing the profound positive changes it can bring!

CHAPTER 3

CREATING A DIGITAL DETOX PLAN

SETTING INTENTIONS
Setting intentions is the first step in creating a successful digital detox plan. It's about understanding why you want to reduce screen time and what you hope to achieve. This chapter will guide you through defining your goals and motivations in a way that is both inspiring and actionable.

IDENTIFY YOUR WHY:Start by asking yourself why you want to reduce your screen time. Are you looking to improve your mental health, strengthen your relationships, or simply have more time for hobbies and interests? Whatever your reasons, writing them down can help clarify your intentions and keep you motivated.

SET CLEAR GOALS:Once you understand your motivations, set specific, achievable goals. Instead of vague resolutions like "spend less time on my phone," aim for concrete objectives such as "reduce social media use to 30 minutes per day" or "no screens after 8 PM." Clear goals give you a target to work towards and make it easier to track your progress.

VISUALIZE SUCCESS:Imagine how your life will improve once you reduce your screen time. Picture yourself feeling more relaxed, enjoying deeper connections with loved ones, and having more time for activities you love. Visualization can be a powerful tool to keep you motivated and committed to your digital detox plan.

COMMIT TO THE PROCESS:Understanding that change takes time and effort. Commit to your goals and be patient with yourself. It's normal to face challenges and setbacks, but with determination and persistence, you can achieve your digital detox objectives.

By setting clear intentions and goals, you lay the foundation for a successful digital detox. This process not only helps you stay focused but also ensures that your efforts are aligned with your values and priorities.

ASSESSING CURRENT USAGE
Before you can effectively reduce your screen time, it's important to understand how much time you're currently spending on your devices and which activities consume the most time. This chapter will introduce you to tools and techniques for tracking your screen time and identifying areas for improvement.

TRACK YOUR SCREEN TIME:Use built-in features on your smartphone or dedicated apps to monitor your screen usage. Apps like Screen Time (iOS) and Digital Wellbeing (Android) provide detailed reports on how much time you spend on different apps and activities. Tracking your usage for a week can give you a clear picture of your habits.

IDENTIFY TIME-WASTERS: Once you have your screen time data, look for patterns and identify the biggest time-wasters. Are you spending hours mindlessly scrolling through social media or getting lost in video recommendations? Knowing where your time goes can help you pinpoint areas for improvement.

REFLECT ON YOUR HABITS:Take some time to reflect on how your screen time makes you feel. Do certain activities leave you feeling drained or stressed? Are there moments when you turn to your phone out of boredom or habit? Understanding the emotional and psychological triggers behind your screen use can help you develop healthier habits.

SET BASELINES AND GOALS: Based on your assessment, set baselines for your current screen time and establish realistic goals for reduction. For example, if you currently spend 4 hours a day on social media, aim to reduce it to 2 hours. Gradual changes are more sustainable and less overwhelming than drastic cuts.

USE TECHNOLOGY WISELY:Leverage technology to help you manage your screen time. Many devices and apps offer features like screen time limits, reminders to take breaks, and focus modes to minimize distractions. Utilize these tools to support your digital detox efforts.

By assessing your current screen usage, you gain valuable insights into your habits and identify specific areas for improvement. This step is crucial for creating a personalized and effective digital detox plan.

CREATING BOUNDARIES

Creating boundaries around your screen use is essential for maintaining a healthy balance between online and offline activities. This chapter will provide practical tips for setting limits on screen usage, including creating tech-free zones and times.

DESIGNATE TECH-FREE ZONES: Establish specific areas in your home where screens are not allowed. Common tech-free zones include the bedroom, dining area, and living room. These spaces should be reserved for rest, relaxation, and meaningful interactions without the interference of screens.

SET TECH-FREE TIMES:Determine certain times of the day when you will disconnect from screens. For example, you might decide to go screen-free during meals, an hour before bedtime, or the first hour after waking up. Consistently adhering to these tech-free times can help you develop healthier habits and routines.

CREATE A SCREEN TIME SCHEDULE:Instead of mindlessly reaching for your devices throughout the day, create a schedule for your screen time. Allocate specific blocks of time for checking emails, browsing social media, or watching videos. Having a structured schedule can prevent overuse and help you stay focused on other activities.

IMPLEMENT DIGITAL DETOX DAYS:Consider dedicating one day a week to a complete digital detox. Use this day to engage in offline activities, spend time with loved ones, or simply relax without screens. Digital detox days can serve as a refreshing reset and reinforce the benefits of unplugging.

COMMUNICATE YOUR BOUNDARIES: Let your family, friends, and colleagues know about your digital detox plan and boundaries. Clear communication can help them understand and respect your intentions. Additionally, having their support can make it easier to stick to your goals.

DEVELOP OFFLINE ALTERNATIVES: Find enjoyable and fulfilling offline activities to replace your screen time. Whether it's reading a book, going for a walk, playing a sport, or picking up a new hobby, having alternative activities can make it easier to reduce your reliance on screens.

Creating boundaries around your screen use is a powerful way to reclaim your time and energy. By establishing tech-free zones and times, scheduling your screen use, and finding fulfilling offline activities, you can create a balanced and enriching digital-free life.

By setting intentions, assessing current usage, and creating boundaries, you can develop a comprehensive and effective digital detox plan. These steps provide a clear and structured approach to reducing screen time and rediscovering the joy of a balanced, fulfilling life. So, let's embark on this journey together and embrace the transformative power of unplugging!

CHAPTER 4

EMBRACING OFFLINE ACTIVITIES

REDISCOVERING HOBBIES
In a world dominated by screens, many of us have lost touch with the hobbies and passions that once brought us joy. Rediscovering these activities can be incredibly rewarding and offer a fulfilling alternative to screen time. Here's how to reconnect with old hobbies and discover new ones:

REVISIT PAST PASSIONS:Think back to activities you enjoyed before screens took over. Did you love painting, playing a musical instrument, gardening, or reading books? Reconnecting with these hobbies can bring a sense of nostalgia and joy. Dust off your old guitar, dig out those art supplies, or visit your local library. You'll be surprised at how much satisfaction you can derive from these simple pleasures.

EXPLORE NEW INTERESTS: If you're looking to try something new, consider exploring activities that don't involve screens. Take up knitting, join a cooking class, learn a new language, or try your hand at pottery. The key is to find something that excites and engages you. Many community centers and local organizations offer classes and workshops that can introduce you to new hobbies and help you meet like-minded individuals.

CREATE A HOBBY SPACE:Designate a specific area in your home for your hobbies. Whether it's a corner for crafting, a nook for reading, or a space for playing music, having a dedicated hobby space can make it easier to engage in these activities regularly. This physical separation from screens can also help reinforce your commitment to spending time offline.

INVOLVE OTHERS:Hobbies can be a great way to connect with others. Invite friends or family members to join you in your activities. Start a book club, host a game night, or join a local sports team. Sharing your hobbies with others can enhance your enjoyment and provide a sense of community.

Rediscovering hobbies not only fills your time with meaningful and enjoyable activities but also provides a much-needed break from screens. By engaging in offline pursuits, you can tap into your creativity, develop new skills, and find joy in the simple things in life.

PHYSICAL ACTIVITIES
Incorporating physical activities into your routine is essential for both physical health and mental well-being. Here's how embracing exercise and outdoor activities can transform your life:

HEALTH BENEFITS:Regular physical activity is crucial for maintaining a healthy body. Exercise helps improve cardiovascular health, strengthens muscles and bones, boosts the immune system, and aids in weight management. It also reduces the risk of chronic diseases such as diabetes, heart disease, and certain cancers. By making physical activity a priority, you invest in your long-term health and well-being.

MENTAL WELL-BEING:Exercise is a powerful tool for improving mental health. Physical activity releases endorphins, the body's natural mood elevators, which can help reduce feelings of stress, anxiety, and depression. Engaging in regular exercise can also improve sleep quality, increase energy levels, and enhance overall cognitive function. Whether it's a brisk walk, a yoga session, or a high-intensity workout, physical activity has profound benefits for your mind and body.

OUTDOOR ADVENTURES: Spending time outdoors has additional benefits beyond exercise. Being in nature can reduce stress, improve mood, and increase feelings of happiness and well-being. Activities like hiking, cycling, swimming, or simply walking in a park allow you to connect with nature and enjoy the beauty of the natural world. Outdoor adventures provide a refreshing break from the digital world and offer a sense of freedom and rejuvenation.

SOCIAL CONNECTIONS: Physical activities can also be a great way to connect with others. Joining a sports team, participating in group fitness classes, or going for a run with a friend can enhance your social interactions and provide a sense of camaraderie. Sharing physical activities with others can make exercise more enjoyable and help you stay motivated.

By embracing physical activities, you can improve your overall health, boost your mood, and find fulfillment in the natural world. Making time for exercise and outdoor adventures is a powerful way to enhance your life and reduce your reliance on screens.

MINDFULNESS AND MEDITATION
Cultivating mindfulness and incorporating meditation into your daily routine can significantly reduce stress and improve your overall well-being. Here's how to embrace these practices:

UNDERSTANDING MINDFULNESS:Mindfulness is the practice of being fully present and engaged in the moment. It involves paying attention to your thoughts, feelings, and surroundings without judgment. Mindfulness can help you become more aware of your screen habits and make conscious choices about how you spend your time.

BENEFITS OF MEDITATION: Meditation is a powerful tool for cultivating mindfulness and reducing stress. Regular meditation practice can help calm the mind, reduce anxiety, and improve focus. It can also enhance emotional regulation and increase feelings of compassion and empathy. By setting aside a few minutes each day for meditation, you can experience profound benefits for your mental and emotional well-being.

SIMPLE MEDITATION TECHNIQUES: If you're new to meditation, start with simple techniques such as focused breathing, body scan, or guided meditation. Find a quiet space, sit comfortably, and focus on your breath. Notice the sensation of each inhale and exhale, and gently bring your attention back to your breath whenever your mind wanders. You can also try guided meditations available through apps or online platforms to help you get started.

INCORPORATE MINDFULNESS INTO DAILY LIFE: Mindfulness doesn't have to be limited to formal meditation practice. You can incorporate mindfulness into your daily activities by paying attention to the present moment. Whether you're eating a meal, taking a walk, or engaging in a conversation, practice being fully present and aware. This can help reduce stress and enhance your overall quality of life.

MINDFULNESS EXERCISES: There are many mindfulness exercises you can try to bring more awareness into your daily routine. Mindful walking, mindful eating, and gratitude journaling are just a few examples. These exercises help you focus on the present moment and cultivate a sense of appreciation and contentment.

Embracing mindfulness and meditation, you can reduce stress, improve your emotional well-being, and find a greater sense of peace and balance. These practices provide a powerful antidote to the constant distractions of the digital world and help you reconnect with yourself and the present moment.

CHAPTER 5

RECONNECTING WITH NATURE

THE HEALING POWER OF NATURE
In our fast-paced, screen-dominated lives, we often forget the profound benefits that nature can offer. Reconnecting with the natural world is not just about spending time outdoors; it's about rediscovering a sense of peace, wonder, and balance. Let's explore the healing power of nature:

PHYSICAL HEALTH BENEFITS: Spending time in nature has been shown to improve physical health. Fresh air, sunlight, and natural surroundings can boost your immune system, lower blood pressure, and increase energy levels. Activities like walking, hiking, or simply sitting in a park can provide gentle exercise that's beneficial for your body.

MENTAL HEALTH BENEFITS: Nature has a calming effect on the mind. Studies have found that spending time in green spaces can reduce stress, anxiety, and depression. The sights, sounds, and smells of nature can soothe the mind and create a sense of tranquility. This is often referred to as "nature therapy" or "ecotherapy."

ENHANCED MOOD AND CREATIVITY:Being in nature can elevate your mood and enhance creativity. The natural environment stimulates the senses and encourages a sense of awe and wonder. This can lead to increased inspiration and a greater ability to think creatively and solve problems.

IMPROVED CONCENTRATION AND FOCUS:Nature can also help improve concentration and focus. Studies have shown that children with

ADHD benefit from spending time in natural settings, as it helps reduce symptoms and improve attention. Similarly, adults can experience enhanced cognitive function and productivity after spending time outdoors.

CONNECTION TO THE EARTH:Reconnecting with nature helps us remember that we are part of a larger ecosystem. This connection can foster a sense of stewardship and responsibility for the environment. Understanding our place in the natural world can inspire us to take better care of our planet and ourselves.

The healing power of nature is profound and multifaceted. By spending more time in natural settings, you can enhance your physical and mental well-being and rediscover a sense of balance and harmony.

OUTDOOR ADVENTURES

Outdoor adventures provide a wonderful opportunity to explore the natural world and engage in activities that are both fun and invigorating. Here are some ideas for outdoor activities that can help you reconnect with nature:

HIKING: Hiking is a great way to explore different landscapes and enjoy the beauty of nature. Whether you prefer gentle trails or challenging climbs, hiking offers physical exercise and a chance to see wildlife and natural scenery up close. Remember to pack essentials like water, snacks, and a map, and always hike with a buddy or let someone know your plans.

CAMPING: Camping allows you to immerse yourself in nature for an extended period. Setting up a tent, cooking over a campfire, and sleeping under the stars can be a rejuvenating experience. Camping trips offer a break from technology and a chance to reconnect with yourself and your surroundings.

BIRDWATCHING: Birdwatching is a relaxing and educational activity that can be done almost anywhere. All you need is a pair of binoculars and a bird guidebook. Take some time to observe and identify different bird species in your area. This activity can help you develop a deeper appreciation for wildlife and the natural world.

GARDENING: Gardening is a rewarding way to connect with nature right in your backyard. Whether you grow flowers, vegetables, or herbs, tending to plants can be a meditative and fulfilling activity. Gardening allows you to observe the cycles of growth and change in nature and can provide a sense of accomplishment.

PICNICKING: Pack a picnic and head to a local park or nature reserve. Enjoying a meal outdoors with family or friends is a simple yet delightful way to spend time in nature. Bring a blanket, some delicious food, and perhaps a good book or some games to enjoy a leisurely day outside.

WATER ACTIVITIES: Activities like kayaking, canoeing, or paddleboarding allow you to explore rivers, lakes, and coastal areas. These water-based adventures offer a unique perspective on the natural world and can be both relaxing and exhilarating.

NATURE WALKS: Sometimes, a simple walk in a local park or nature trail can be just as refreshing as a more strenuous hike. Nature walks allow you to observe the flora and fauna, listen to the sounds of nature, and clear your mind. Take your time and savor the experience.

Engaging in outdoor adventures can help you reconnect with the natural world, provide physical exercise, and offer a refreshing break from screens. These activities are not only enjoyable but also beneficial for your overall well-being.

CREATING A NATURE ROUTINE**
Incorporating nature into your daily life doesn't have to be complicated. By creating a nature routine, you can enjoy the benefits of the outdoors regularly and make it a consistent part of your lifestyle. Here are some tips for establishing a nature routine:

START SMALL: Begin by incorporating small doses of nature into your daily routine. This could be as simple as taking a short walk in a nearby park, having your morning coffee on the patio, or tending to houseplants. Even a few minutes spent outdoors can have a positive impact on your mood and well-being.

SET REGULAR TIMES:Schedule specific times for outdoor activities each week. For example, you might designate Saturday mornings for hiking or Tuesday afternoons for gardening. Having a regular schedule helps ensure that you make time for nature, even on busy days.

CREATE TECH-FREE ZONES:Designate certain areas of your home and yard as tech-free zones. These could include a garden, balcony, or a cozy outdoor nook. Use these spaces for relaxation, meditation, or reading. By creating tech-free zones, you establish a sanctuary where you can unwind and connect with nature.

COMBINE ACTIVITIES: Look for ways to combine nature with other activities. For instance, you can practice yoga or meditation outdoors, have meetings or study sessions in a park, or enjoy meals outside. Integrating nature into your daily activities makes it easier to spend more time outdoors.

PLAN NATURE GETAWAYS:Schedule regular nature getaways, such as weekend camping trips, beach outings, or visits to national parks. These mini-vacations provide a more immersive nature experience and allow you to fully disconnect from screens and technology.

INVOLVE OTHERS: Encourage family and friends to join you in your nature routine. Plan group hikes, picnics, or outdoor games. Sharing these experiences with loved ones can enhance your enjoyment and create lasting memories.

MINDFUL OBSERVATION: Practice mindful observation when you're outdoors. Take time to notice the details of your surroundings—the colors, sounds, and scents of nature. This mindfulness practice can deepen your connection to the natural world and enhance your overall experience.

SEASONAL ACTIVITIES:Embrace seasonal activities that connect you with nature. In the spring, plant a garden or go flower picking. In the summer, enjoy beach days and outdoor sports. In the fall, go apple picking or take scenic drives to see the foliage. In the winter, try snowshoeing, ice skating, or simply enjoy a walk in the snow.

By creating a nature routine, you can make nature a regular and meaningful part of your life. This routine not only provides a refreshing break from screens but also enhances your physical and mental well-being. Embrace the beauty and tranquility of the natural world, and let it enrich your life every day.

Reconnecting with nature offers a multitude of benefits for your mind, body, and spirit. By exploring the healing power of nature, engaging in outdoor adventures, and creating a nature routine, you can rediscover the joy and fulfillment that comes from spending time in the natural world. So, step outside, breathe in the fresh air, and let nature rejuvenate and inspire you!

CHAPTER 6

Enhancing Real-World Connection

Building Stronger Relationships
In an era dominated by digital communication, our real-world connections often suffer. Enhancing these relationships is crucial for our emotional well-being and overall happiness. Here are some strategies for improving communication and deepening connections with family and friends:

PRIORITIZE QUALITY TIME:Make a conscious effort to spend quality time with your loved ones. This means being fully present and engaged during interactions. Set aside dedicated time for family dinners, weekend outings, or just catching up over coffee. The key is to focus on meaningful, uninterrupted interactions that foster a sense of closeness.

ACTIVE LISTENING: One of the most effective ways to improve communication is by practicing active listening. This involves giving your full attention to the speaker, maintaining eye contact, and responding thoughtfully. Show genuine interest in what they're saying, ask questions, and avoid interrupting. Active listening helps build trust and understanding in your relationships.

EXPRESS APPRECIATION: Regularly expressing appreciation and gratitude can strengthen your relationships. Acknowledge the efforts and qualities of your family and friends. Simple gestures like saying "thank you," writing a heartfelt note, or giving a compliment can go a long way in making others feel valued and loved.

BE VULNERABLE: Sharing your thoughts and feelings openly can deepen your connections with others. Don't be afraid to be vulnerable and express your emotions. This fosters a sense of intimacy and trust. Encourage your loved ones to do the same by creating a safe and supportive environment where they feel comfortable opening up.

RESOLVE CONFLICTS RESPECTFULLY: Disagreements are a natural part of any relationship. The key is to address conflicts respectfully and constructively. Approach disagreements with a calm and open mind, listen to the other person's perspective, and work together to find a solution. Avoid blame and focus on understanding and resolving the issue.

SHARED ACTIVITIES: Engage in activities that you and your loved ones enjoy together. Whether it's cooking, hiking, playing board games, or attending events, shared experiences can strengthen your bond and create lasting memories. The joy of doing something together often enhances the quality of your relationship.

By prioritizing quality time, practicing active listening, expressing appreciation, being vulnerable, resolving conflicts respectfully, and engaging in shared activities, you can build stronger, more meaningful relationships with your family and friends.

COMMUNITY ENGAGEMENT
Participating in community activities and volunteering is essential for fostering a sense of belonging and making a positive impact. Here's why community engagement is important and how you can get involved:

SENSE OF BELONGING:Being part of a community gives you a sense of belonging and connection. It helps you feel that you're part of something bigger than yourself. Engaging with your community can provide emotional support, reduce feelings of isolation, and enhance your overall well-being.

BUIILDING RELATIONSHIPS: Community activities and volunteering offer opportunities to meet new people and build relationships. Whether you're attending local events, joining clubs, or participating in group activities, you can connect with like-minded individuals who share your interests and values.

PERSONAL GROWTH:Community engagement allows you to learn new skills, gain new experiences, and grow as a person. Volunteering, in particular, can provide valuable opportunities for personal and professional development. It can enhance your sense of purpose and fulfillment by contributing to a cause you care about.

MAKING A DIFFERENCE: Volunteering and participating in community activities enable you to make a positive impact on others' lives. Whether you're helping out at a local shelter, organizing community clean-ups, or supporting local events, your efforts can create a ripple effect of positive change in your community.

HOW TO GET INVOLVED:There are many ways to engage with your community. Look for local organizations, clubs, and groups that align with your interests and values. Attend community meetings, events, and workshops to stay informed and get involved. Volunteering opportunities are often available through non-profits, schools, and community centers. Choose activities that resonate with you and fit your schedule.

By actively engaging in your community and volunteering, you can foster a sense of belonging, build meaningful relationships, grow personally, and make a positive difference. Community engagement enriches your life and enhances your connection to the world around you.

SOCIALIZING WITHOUT SCREENS
In our digital age, it's easy to rely on technology for socializing. However, face-to-face interactions offer a deeper and more fulfilling way to connect with others. Here are some fun and engaging ways to socialize without screens:

HOST GATHERINGS:Organize gatherings with family and friends, such as game nights, dinner parties, or potlucks. Encourage everyone to leave their devices at the door and focus on enjoying each other's company. These gatherings provide an opportunity for meaningful conversations, laughter, and bonding.

OUTDOOR ACTIVITIES: Plan outdoor activities that allow you to socialize while enjoying nature. Go for a hike, have a picnic in the park, or play sports like soccer, tennis, or frisbee. Outdoor activities provide a refreshing change of scenery and can be a great way to spend quality time together.

WORKSHOPS AND CLASSES: Attend workshops and classes that interest you, such as cooking, painting, dancing, or yoga. These settings offer a chance to meet new people with similar interests and learn something new together. Engaging in hands-on activities can foster a sense of camaraderie and connection.

COMMUNITY EVENTS: Participate in local community events, such as festivals, farmers' markets, and fairs. These events provide a vibrant and social atmosphere where you can interact with others and enjoy shared experiences. Support local vendors, try new foods, and enjoy the entertainment.

BOARD GAMES AND PUZZLES:Bring back the joy of traditional games and puzzles. Gather your friends and family for a board game night or work on a challenging puzzle together. These activities encourage teamwork, strategic thinking, and lots of fun without the need for screens.

EXERCISE TOGETHER:Join a fitness class, go for a group run, or take a dance class with friends. Exercising together is not only healthy but also a great way to motivate each other and build strong bonds. The shared experience of working towards fitness goals can enhance your relationships.

BOOK CLUBS:Start or join a book club where you can discuss literature and share your thoughts on various books. Book clubs offer a platform for engaging discussions and intellectual stimulation. They also provide a structured way to socialize regularly.

VOLUNTEER TOGETHER:Volunteering as a group can be a rewarding way to spend time with others. Choose a cause you're passionate about and volunteer your time and skills together. This shared experience can deepen your connections and create lasting memories.

By hosting gatherings, planning outdoor activities, attending workshops and classes, participating in community events, playing board games and puzzles, exercising together, joining book clubs, and volunteering, you can enjoy socializing in a more meaningful and engaging way without screens. These activities foster real-world connections that are fulfilling and enriching.

Enhancing real-world connections involves building stronger relationships, engaging with your community, and finding ways to socialize without screens. By focusing on these areas, you can cultivate deeper, more meaningful connections and enjoy the richness of human interaction. So, step away from the screens, embrace the real world, and let your relationships thrive!

CHAPTER 7

Digital Minimalism

THE PRINCIPLES OF DIGITAL MINIMALISM

Digital Minimalism is a philosophy that advocates for a more intentional and thoughtful approach to technology use. It's about reclaiming control over your digital life and focusing on what truly matters. Here's an in-depth look at the principles of Digital Minimalism and how they can simplify your life:

INTENTIONAL USE:At the core of Digital Minimalism is the idea of intentionality. Rather than mindlessly scrolling through social media or getting lost in a sea of notifications, Digital Minimalism encourages you to be deliberate about how you use technology. This means asking yourself why you're using a particular app or platform and what value it brings to your life.

QUALITY OVER QUANTITY:Digital Minimalism emphasizes quality interactions over the sheer quantity of digital engagements. It's about choosing to spend your time on meaningful online activities that enrich your life, rather than being overwhelmed by a constant stream of trivial content.

FOCUSED ATTENTION: This principle involves prioritizing deep work and focused attention. Digital Minimalism encourages you to set aside dedicated time for important tasks without the distraction of technology. By doing so, you can achieve greater productivity and a sense of accomplishment.

DIGITAL DECLUTTERING: Simplifying your digital life by decluttering your devices, apps, and online presence is another key principle. This involves removing unnecessary digital clutter that doesn't serve a purpose, allowing you to focus on what's truly important.

MINDFUL CONSUMPTION: Digital Minimalism promotes mindful consumption of digital content. Instead of passively consuming information, it encourages you to engage actively and thoughtfully. This means being selective about the media you consume and ensuring it aligns with your values and goals.

By embracing the principles of Digital Minimalism, you can simplify your digital life, reduce stress, and create more space for meaningful activities and relationships.

CURATING YOUR DIGITAL SPACE

Curating your digital space involves organizing and optimizing your digital environment to support a more balanced and fulfilling life. Here are some tips for decluttering your digital life, including email, social media, and apps:

EMAIL MANAGEMENT:
1. UNSUBSCRIBE: Start by unsubscribing from newsletters and promotional emails that no longer interest you. Use tools like Unroll.Me to streamline this process.
2. FOLDERS AND LABELS: Organize your inbox with folders and labels to keep track of important emails. Create categories for work, personal, and other relevant areas.
3. EMAIL RULES: Set up email rules to automatically sort incoming messages. This helps keep your inbox clean and ensures important emails don't get lost.
4. REGULAR CLEAN-UP: Schedule regular times to clean up your inbox. Delete or archive old emails and ensure your inbox stays manageable.

SOCIAL MEDIA:

1. AUDIT YOUR ACCOUNTS: Review your social media accounts and unfollow or unfriend individuals, pages, or groups that don't add value to your life.

2. LIMIT NOTIFICATIONS: Turn off unnecessary notifications to reduce distractions. Only keep notifications for essential updates.

3. SCHEDULED USAGE: Set specific times for checking social media rather than constantly checking throughout the day. This helps maintain focus and reduces screen time.

4. POSITIVE CONTENT:Follow accounts that inspire and uplift you. Curate your feed to reflect your interests and values.

APPS AND DEVICES:

1. APP AUDIT: Go through your devices and delete apps that you no longer use or need. This frees up space and reduces digital clutter.

2. ESSENTIAL APPS ONLY:Keep only essential apps on your home screen and organize the rest into folders. This makes your device easier to navigate and reduces distractions.

3. USAGE TRACKING: Use built-in tools or third-party apps to track your app usage. This can help you identify areas where you might be spending too much time.

4. DIGITAL DETOX TOOLS: Utilize digital wellness tools to set limits on app usage and screen time. These tools can help you maintain a healthier relationship with technology.

By curating your digital space, you create an environment that supports your well-being and allows you to focus on what truly matters. This process helps you regain control over your digital life and reduces the overwhelm caused by excessive digital clutter.

SUSTAINABLE DIGITAL PRACTICES

Maintaining a balanced approach to technology use in the long term requires sustainable digital practices. Here's how you can cultivate a healthier relationship with technology:

SET CLEAR BOUNDARIES:
1. TECH-FREE ZONES:Designate certain areas of your home as tech-free zones, such as the dining room or bedroom. This encourages you to be present and engage in non-digital activities.
2. TECH-FREE TIMES:Establish specific times of the day when you disconnect from technology, such as during meals or before bedtime. This helps you create a routine that includes regular breaks from screens.

PURPOSEFUL USE
1. DEFINE YOUR GOALS:Clearly define your goals and intentions for using technology. Whether it's for work, learning, or connecting with others, having a clear purpose helps you stay focused and avoid mindless use.
2. PRIORITIZE MEANINGFUL ACTIVITIES: Focus on using technology for activities that align with your values and contribute to your well-being. This might include online learning, creative projects, or connecting with loved ones.

MINDFUL CONSUMPTION:
1. CURATE YOUR CONTENT: Be selective about the digital content you consume. Follow accounts and subscribe to channels that provide value and resonate with your interests.
2. LIMIT MULTITASKING: Avoid multitasking with multiple devices or apps. Focus on one task at a time to enhance productivity and reduce cognitive overload.

REGULAR REFLECTION:
1. ASSESS YOUR USAGE: Periodically assess your technology use and its impact on your life. Reflect on whether it aligns with your goals and values and make adjustments as needed.

2. SET REALISTIC LIMITS: Set realistic limits on screen time and app usage. Use tools like screen time reports to monitor your habits and make informed decisions.

EMBRACE OFFLINE ACTIVITIES:
1. HOBBIES AND INTERESTS: Engage in hobbies and interests that don't involve screens. This could include reading, gardening, painting, or playing a musical instrument.
2. OUTDOOR ACTIVITIES:Spend time outdoors and enjoy nature. Activities like hiking, biking, or simply taking a walk can provide a refreshing break from screens.

By adopting sustainable digital practices, you can maintain a balanced and healthy relationship with technology. These practices help you stay focused, reduce stress, and create more space for meaningful offline activities and connections.

Digital Minimalism offers a transformative approach to technology use by emphasizing intentionality, quality interactions, and mindful consumption. By curating your digital space and adopting sustainable digital practices, you can simplify your life, reduce digital overwhelm, and create a healthier, more balanced lifestyle. Embrace the principles of Digital Minimalism and rediscover the joy and fulfillment that come from a more intentional and thoughtful approach to technology.

CHAPTER 8

NAVIGATING WORK AND TECHNOLOGY

BALANCING WORK AND LIFE

In today's digital world, maintaining a healthy work-life balance can be challenging. The constant connectivity often blurs the lines between work and personal life. However, with the right strategies, you can achieve a balanced and fulfilling life. Here are some effective strategies to help you maintain a healthy work-life balance:

SET CLEAR BOUNDARIES: One of the most important steps in achieving work-life balance is setting clear boundaries between work and personal time. Establish specific work hours and stick to them. Communicate these boundaries to your colleagues and family members to ensure everyone respects your time. Avoid checking work emails or taking business calls outside of your designated work hours.

PRIORITIZE TASKS: Use a task management system to prioritize your tasks based on their importance and urgency. Break down large tasks into smaller, manageable steps and tackle them one at a time. This helps you stay focused and prevents you from feeling overwhelmed. Make sure to include time for personal activities and relaxation in your daily schedule.

TAKE REGULAR BREAKS:Taking regular breaks throughout your workday is essential for maintaining productivity and reducing stress. Use techniques like the Pomodoro Technique, where you work for 25 minutes and then take a 5-minute break. During your breaks, step away from your screen, stretch, take a walk, or engage in a relaxing activity.

DISCONNECT AFTER WORK:Once your workday is over, make a conscious effort to disconnect from work-related activities. This means turning off work notifications, closing your laptop, and avoiding work-related discussions. Use this time to unwind, spend quality time with loved ones, and engage in activities that bring you joy and relaxation.

PLAN PERSONAL ACTIVITIES:Schedule personal activities and hobbies that you enjoy. Whether it's exercising, reading, cooking, or spending time with friends and family, make sure to allocate time for these activities in your daily or weekly routine. This helps you recharge and prevents burnout.

PRACTICE SELF-CARE: Taking care of your physical and mental well-being is crucial for maintaining a healthy work-life balance. Make time for regular exercise, healthy eating, and sufficient sleep. Practice mindfulness and relaxation techniques, such as meditation or deep breathing exercises, to reduce stress and improve your overall well-being.

By setting clear boundaries, prioritizing tasks, taking regular breaks, disconnecting after work, planning personal activities, and practicing self-care, you can achieve a healthy work-life balance and enjoy a more fulfilling life.

PRODUCTIVITY HACKS

Staying productive without being constantly tethered to screens requires adopting effective productivity hacks that help you manage your time and tasks efficiently. Here are some practical tips to boost your productivity:

THE POMODORO TECHNIQUE:This time management method involves working in focused intervals (usually 25 minutes) followed by short breaks (5 minutes). After completing four intervals, take a longer break (15-30 minutes). This technique helps maintain focus, prevent burnout, and increase productivity.

TASK BATCHING: Group similar tasks together and tackle them in batches. For example, set aside specific times for checking emails, making phone calls, or completing administrative tasks. Task batching reduces context switching and allows you to work more efficiently.

USE A TO-DO LIST: Create a daily to-do list to organize your tasks and prioritize them based on importance and urgency. Use digital tools like Trello, Asana, or Todoist, or stick to a simple paper list. Regularly review and update your list to stay on track and ensure you're focusing on the most important tasks.

LIMIT DISTRACTIONS:Identify and minimize distractions in your work environment. This might involve turning off unnecessary notifications, closing non-essential tabs, and setting specific times for checking emails and social media. Create a dedicated workspace that is free from distractions to help you stay focused.

SET CLEAR GOALS: Define clear, achievable goals for your work. Break larger projects into smaller, manageable tasks and set deadlines for each. Having clear goals helps you stay motivated and focused, and provides a sense of accomplishment as you complete each task.

TIME BLOCKING: Allocate specific blocks of time for different tasks and activities throughout your day. This technique helps you manage your time effectively and ensures you're dedicating sufficient time to each task. Include time blocks for breaks and personal activities to maintain a balanced schedule.

PRACTICE MINDFULNESS: Incorporate mindfulness techniques into your daily routine to improve focus and reduce stress. Techniques like meditation, deep breathing, and mindful walking can help you stay present and maintain a clear mind, enhancing your productivity.

By adopting these productivity hacks, you can manage your time more effectively, stay focused, and achieve your goals without being constantly tethered to screens.

TECH-FREE WORKSPACES

Creating a tech-free workspace can significantly enhance your focus and productivity by minimizing distractions and fostering a conducive work environment. Here are some tips for setting up a tech-free workspace:

DESIGNATE A SPECIFIC AREA:Choose a specific area in your home or office for your tech-free workspace. This could be a separate room, a corner of a room, or even a specific desk. The key is to have a dedicated space where you can work without digital distractions.

MINIMIZE DIGITAL DEVICES: Remove or minimize the presence of digital devices in your tech-free workspace. Keep your smartphone, tablet, and other gadgets out of sight or in another room. Use analog tools like a notebook, planner, or physical calendar to organize your tasks and schedule.

USE ANALOG TOOLS:Equip your tech-free workspace with analog tools such as pens, notebooks, sticky notes, and a whiteboard. These tools can help you brainstorm, jot down ideas, and organize your tasks without relying on digital devices.

CREATE A CALMING ENVIRONMENT:Make your tech-free workspace inviting and conducive to focus. Use comfortable furniture, good lighting, and decor that inspires you. Plants, artwork, and natural light can create a calming atmosphere that enhances your productivity.

SET BOUNDARIES: Establish clear boundaries for your tech-free workspace. Communicate with family members or colleagues to ensure they respect your tech-free zone. Set specific times for using this space and stick to your schedule to maintain consistency.

INCORPORATE BREAKS: Integrate regular breaks into your work routine to prevent burnout and maintain focus. Use these breaks to step away from your tech-free workspace, stretch, take a walk, or engage in a relaxing activity. This helps you recharge and return to work with renewed energy.

PRACTICE MINDFULNESS:Use mindfulness techniques to stay present and focused while working in your tech-free workspace. Deep breathing exercises, meditation, and mindful stretching can help you clear your mind and maintain concentration.

By creating a tech-free workspace and incorporating analog tools, you can minimize distractions, enhance your focus, and create a productive work environment. This approach allows you to maintain a healthy balance between technology use and real-world activities, ultimately improving your work-life balance and overall well-being.

Navigating work and technology involves balancing work and life, adopting productivity hacks, and creating tech-free workspaces. By implementing these strategies, you can achieve a healthier, more balanced approach to technology use, enhance your productivity, and enjoy a more fulfilling life. Embrace these principles and discover the benefits of a more intentional and thoughtful approach to work and technology.

CHAPTER 9

MINDFUL TECHNOLOGY USE

CONSCIOUS CONSUMPTION

In a world saturated with digital content, being intentional about what you consume can significantly impact your mental well-being and productivity. Conscious consumption means actively choosing media and content that add value to your life rather than passively absorbing whatever comes your way. Here's how you can practice conscious consumption:

EVALUATE YOUR CONTENT SOURCES:Start by evaluating the sources of your digital content. Whether it's news, social media, podcasts, or videos, assess whether these sources align with your values and goals. Follow creators and platforms that inspire, educate, and uplift you. Unsubscribe from those that provoke stress, anxiety, or negativity.

SET CLEAR GOALS:Define what you want to gain from your digital consumption. Are you looking to learn a new skill, stay informed about current events, or simply entertain yourself? Having clear goals helps you make more deliberate choices about what content to engage with and for how long.

LIMIT EXPOSURE TO NEGATIVE CONTENT:Be mindful of the emotional impact of the content you consume. Avoid sources that focus on fear, anger, or sensationalism. Instead, seek out positive, constructive, and solution-oriented content. This shift can improve your mood and overall mental health.

QUALITY OVER QUANTITY:Focus on consuming high-quality content rather than a high quantity of content. This means choosing in-depth articles over clickbait, thoughtful documentaries over mindless reality TV, and meaningful conversations over superficial social media interactions.

SCHEDULE CONSUMPTION TIME: Allocate specific times for consuming digital content, just as you would for any other activity. This prevents you from falling into the trap of endless scrolling and ensures that your consumption is intentional and balanced with other activities.

By practicing conscious consumption, you can curate a digital experience that enhances your life, supports your goals, and contributes to your well-being. This mindful approach to media and content consumption helps you reclaim control over your digital life.

MINDFUL USAGE HABITS

Staying present and aware while using technology can prevent mindless usage and promote a healthier relationship with your digital devices. Here are some techniques for cultivating mindful usage habits:

SET INTENTIONS BEFORE USE:Before you pick up your phone or open your laptop, set a clear intention for what you want to achieve. Whether it's sending an email, checking the news, or watching a tutorial, having a purpose helps you stay focused and avoid getting sidetracked.

PRACTICE THE "PAUSE AND REFLECT " METHOD: When you feel the urge to check your phone or browse the internet, pause and reflect for a moment. Ask yourself if this action aligns with your current goals and needs. This brief pause can help you make more deliberate choices about your technology use.

LIMIT MULTITASKING: Avoid using multiple devices or apps simultaneously. Multitasking can reduce your efficiency and increase stress.

Instead, focus on one task at a time, giving it your full attention. This approach enhances your productivity and allows you to be fully present.

USE TECHNOLOGY MINDFULLY:Engage with technology in a way that enhances your awareness and presence. For example, when reading an article, focus entirely on the content without switching tabs or checking notifications. When using social media, interact thoughtfully rather than mindlessly scrolling.

SET DIGITAL BOUNDARIES:Establish clear boundaries for when and where you use technology. For instance, designate certain times of day as screen-free periods, such as during meals or an hour before bed. Create tech-free zones in your home, like the dining room or bedroom, to encourage more mindful interactions.

INCORPORATE MINDFULNESS PRACTICES: Integrate mindfulness practices into your daily routine to enhance your overall awareness. Techniques such as deep breathing, meditation, and mindful walking can help you stay grounded and present, even when using technology.

By adopting these mindful usage habits, you can cultivate a more intentional and balanced relationship with technology. This approach helps you stay focused, reduce stress, and create more meaningful digital interactions.

DIGITAL DETOX RETREATS

Taking extended breaks from technology through digital detox retreats can provide profound benefits for your mental and physical well-being. Here's how to understand the benefits and plan your own digital detox retreat:

THE BENEFITS OF DIGITAL DETOX RETREATS:

1. MENTAL CLARITY: Stepping away from screens allows your mind to rest and reset. Without the constant barrage of information and notifications, you can experience greater mental clarity and improved focus.

2. REDUCED STRESS AND ANXIETY: Disconnecting from digital devices reduces the stress and anxiety often associated with constant connectivity. It provides an opportunity to relax, unwind, and reconnect with yourself.

3. ENHANCED RELATIONSHIPS: Spending time offline allows you to engage more deeply with the people around you. Without digital distractions, you can enjoy more meaningful conversations and strengthen your relationships.

4. INCREASED CREATIVITY: A digital detox can stimulate your creativity by providing the mental space needed for new ideas and inspirations to emerge. Without the noise of digital content, you can tap into your creative potential.

5. IMPROVED PHYSICAL HEALTH: Reducing screen time can have positive effects on your physical health, such as better sleep, reduced eye strain, and more time for physical activities.

HOW TO PLAN A DIGITAL DETOX RETREAT:

1. CHOOSE A LOCATION: Select a location that supports your goal of disconnecting from technology. This could be a remote cabin, a beach house, a campsite, or even a staycation at home with strict no-screen rules. Ensure the environment is conducive to relaxation and minimal distractions.

2. SET CLEAR GOALS: Define what you hope to achieve during your digital detox retreat. Whether it's reducing stress, reconnecting with nature, or spending quality time with loved ones, having clear goals will guide your activities and intentions.

3. INFORM OTHERS: Let your friends, family, and colleagues know about your digital detox retreat in advance. Inform them of your plans to be offline and provide alternative ways to reach you in case of emergencies.

4. PREPARE ACTIVITIES: Plan activities that don't involve screens, such as hiking, reading, journaling, meditating, practicing yoga, cooking, or engaging in creative hobbies. Bring along books, art supplies, board games, or musical instruments to keep yourself entertained.

5. ESTABLISH RULES: Set clear rules for your digital detox retreat. This might include turning off all digital devices, leaving them in a designated spot, or only using them for emergencies. Stick to these rules to ensure you fully experience the benefits of the detox.

6. REFLECT AND JOURNAL:Use this time to reflect on your relationship with technology and its impact on your life. Keep a journal to document your thoughts, feelings, and experiences during the retreat. This can provide valuable insights and help you maintain a healthier balance when you return to your digital routine.

By planning and committing to a digital detox retreat, you can experience the profound benefits of disconnecting from technology and reconnecting with yourself and the world around you. This intentional break from screens can lead to greater mental clarity, reduced stress, and enhanced well-being.

Mindful technology use involves conscious consumption, mindful usage habits, and digital detox retreats. By embracing these practices, you can create a healthier, more balanced relationship with technology. This approach allows you to enjoy the benefits of digital connectivity while maintaining your well-being and enhancing your real-world experiences. Embrace mindful technology use and discover the joy and fulfillment that come from a more intentional and thoughtful approach to digital life.

CHAPTER 10

LONG-TERM SUCCESS

MAINTAINING MOMENTUM

Staying motivated and committed to a digital-free lifestyle can be challenging, especially in a world where technology is so deeply ingrained in our daily lives. However, with the right strategies, you can maintain momentum and continue reaping the benefits of reduced screen time. Here are some effective ways to stay motivated and committed:

SET CLEAR GOALS AND REMINDERS:Clearly define your goals for a digital-free lifestyle. Whether it's improving your mental health, strengthening relationships, or enhancing productivity, having clear goals helps you stay focused. Use reminders, such as sticky notes or alarms, to keep these goals front and center in your daily life.

CREATE A SUPPORT SYSTEM:Surround yourself with supportive friends, family members, or communities who share your commitment to reducing screen time. Share your goals and progress with them, and seek their encouragement and accountability. Join online or local groups focused on digital minimalism or technology detox to connect with like-minded individuals.

TRACK YOUR PROGRESS: Keep a journal or use a tracking app to monitor your screen time and document your digital-free activities. Tracking your progress provides a sense of accomplishment and helps you identify patterns or areas for improvement. Celebrate small victories and milestones along the way.

REGULARLY REVIEW AND ADJUST:Periodically review your digital habits and goals. Assess what's working well and what needs adjustment. Be flexible and willing to adapt your approach as needed. This ongoing evaluation helps you stay on track and maintain a balanced relationship with technology.

FIND ALTERNATIVES: Identify and engage in fulfilling activities that don't involve screens. Rediscover hobbies, spend time outdoors, practice mindfulness, or learn new skills. Finding enjoyable alternatives makes it easier to stick to your digital-free lifestyle and reduces the temptation to revert to old habits.

STAY INSPIRED:Read books, watch documentaries, or listen to podcasts about digital minimalism, mindfulness, and personal growth. Surrounding yourself with inspiring content keeps you motivated and reinforces the benefits of reducing screen time.

By setting clear goals, creating a support system, tracking your progress, regularly reviewing and adjusting, finding alternatives, and staying inspired, you can maintain momentum and stay committed to a digital-free lifestyle. This ongoing commitment leads to long-term benefits and a more fulfilling life.

CELEBRATING PROGRESS

Recognizing and celebrating your achievements along the way is crucial for maintaining motivation and reinforcing positive behavior. Here are some ways to celebrate your progress and stay motivated:

ACKNOWLEDGE SMALL WINS:Celebrate even the smallest achievements, such as completing a day without checking social media or spending an entire afternoon engaged in a screen-free activity. Acknowledging these small wins builds momentum and keeps you motivated.

REWARD YOURSELF: Treat yourself to rewards for reaching milestones or sticking to your digital-free goals. Rewards can be simple, like enjoying a favorite treat, taking a relaxing bath, or spending time doing something you love. Positive reinforcement makes the journey more enjoyable and rewarding.

REFLECT ON YOUR ACHIEVEMENTS: Take time to reflect on your progress and how it has positively impacted your life. Write down the benefits you've experienced, such as improved mental clarity, better relationships, or enhanced well-being. Reflecting on these positive changes reinforces your commitment and motivation.

SHARE YOUR SUCCESS: Share your achievements with friends, family, or your support group. Celebrating together amplifies the joy and encourages others to join you in your digital-free journey. Sharing your success also provides accountability and further motivation.

CREATE A VISUAL REPRESENTATION: Use a visual tool, such as a progress chart or vision board, to track and celebrate your achievements. Seeing your progress visually can be highly motivating and serves as a constant reminder of how far you've come.

CELEBRATE MILESTONES:Plan special celebrations for reaching significant milestones, such as completing a week or month of reduced screen time. Celebrate these milestones with meaningful activities, such as a day trip, a special dinner, or a gathering with loved ones.

By acknowledging small wins, rewarding yourself, reflecting on your achievements, sharing your success, creating a visual representation, and celebrating milestones, you can maintain a positive and motivated mindset. Celebrating progress reinforces your commitment and makes the journey more enjoyable.

INSPIRING OTHERS

Sharing your journey and inspiring others to embrace a digital-free life can amplify the positive impact of your efforts and create a supportive community. Here's how you can inspire others:

LEAD BY EXAMPLE: The most powerful way to inspire others is by leading by example. Demonstrate the benefits of a digital-free lifestyle through your actions and behaviors. Share your experiences, challenges, and successes openly and authentically.

SHARE YOUR STORY: Use various platforms, such as social media, blogs, or public speaking, to share your digital-free journey. Highlight the positive changes you've experienced and provide practical tips and advice for others looking to reduce their screen time. Your story can resonate with and motivate others to take similar steps.

ENCOURAGE OPEN CONVERSATIONS: Initiate conversations about the impact of technology on well-being and the benefits of a digital-free lifestyle. Encourage open and honest discussions with friends, family, and colleagues. Sharing perspectives and experiences can create a supportive environment and inspire others to consider their own digital habits.

OFFER SUPPORT AND RESOURCES:Provide support and resources to those interested in reducing their screen time. Share books, articles, documentaries, and apps that have helped you on your journey. Offer to be a mentor or accountability partner for someone looking to make similar changes.

CREATE A COMMUNITY:Organize or join local or online communities focused on digital minimalism or technology detox. Creating a sense of community fosters mutual support, accountability, and inspiration. Participate in group activities, challenges, or events that promote a digital-free lifestyle.

CELEBRATE COLLECTIVE ACHIEVEMENTS:Recognize and celebrate the achievements of others who are also embracing a digital-free life. Share their stories and successes within your community. Collective celebrations create a positive and motivating atmosphere that encourages everyone to continue their efforts.

By leading by example, sharing your story, encouraging open conversations, offering support and resources, creating a community, and celebrating collective achievements, you can inspire others to embrace a digital-free life. Your journey can have a ripple effect, positively impacting those around you and fostering a culture of mindful technology use.

Long-term success in maintaining a digital-free lifestyle involves maintaining momentum, celebrating progress, and inspiring others. By adopting these strategies, you can stay motivated, recognize your achievements, and create a supportive community that encourages mindful technology use. Embrace these principles and discover the lasting benefits of a balanced and intentional approach to digital life.

CONCLUSION

As we reach the conclusion of "Unplugged: Rediscovering Joy in a Digital-Free Life," it's essential to reflect on the journey we've taken together. Embracing a balanced life is not about completely rejecting technology but about using it mindfully and finding harmony between our digital and offline worlds. This final chapter will summarize the key takeaways and inspire you to continue on this path toward a more fulfilling, balanced life.

REFLECTING ON THE JOURNEY

Throughout this book, we've explored various aspects of how screens and technology impact our lives. We've delved into the science behind screen time, recognized the signs of digital dependence, and uncovered the many benefits of unplugging. We've also discussed practical strategies for reducing screen time, creating digital detox plans, and embracing offline activities. Now, let's tie everything together.

A NEW PERSPECTIVE:By understanding the ubiquity of screens and the science of screen time, you've gained a new perspective on how pervasive technology is in our daily lives. Recognizing digital dependence and its effects on our mental and physical health has provided you with the insight needed to make meaningful changes.

EMPOWERMENT THROUGH KNOWLEDGE:Knowledge is power, and throughout this journey, you've equipped yourself with the tools and strategies to take control of your digital habits. Whether it's setting boundaries, practicing mindful technology use, or engaging in digital detox retreats, you now have a robust toolkit to help you maintain a balanced life.

CELEBRATING PROGRESS: It's crucial to acknowledge and celebrate the progress you've made. Every small step, from reducing screen time to engaging in new hobbies, is a victory. These achievements are a testament to your commitment and resilience in pursuing a healthier, more balanced lifestyle.

THE IMPORTANCE OF BALANCE

Balance is the cornerstone of a fulfilling life. While technology brings many conveniences and benefits, it's vital to balance its use with activities that enrich our offline experiences. Here's how you can continue to embrace a balanced life:

INTENTIONAL TECHNOLOGY USE:Use technology intentionally and mindfully. Ask yourself if each interaction with your device serves a meaningful purpose. By being deliberate in your technology use, you can ensure that it enhances rather than detracts from your life.

PRIORITIZE REAL-WORLD CONNECTIONS: Invest in real-world relationships and activities. Spend quality time with loved ones, engage in face-to-face conversations, and participate in community events. These connections are crucial for your emotional well-being and provide a sense of belonging and fulfillment.

INCORPORATING OFFLINE ACTIVITIES:Continuously seek out and engage in offline activities that bring you joy and satisfaction. Whether it's rediscovering old hobbies, exploring nature, or practicing mindfulness, these activities are essential for maintaining a balanced and enriching life.

REGULAR DIGITAL DETOXES:Make digital detoxes a regular part of your routine. Periodic breaks from screens allow you to reset and recharge, fostering mental clarity and reducing stress. These detoxes can range from a few hours each day to extended retreats, depending on your needs and lifestyle.

INSPIRING ONGOING CHANGE

Embracing a balanced life is an ongoing journey, not a one-time event. Here's how you can continue to inspire change in yourself and others:

LEAD BY EXAMPLE: Your actions can inspire those around you. By demonstrating the benefits of a balanced, digital-free lifestyle, you encourage others to consider their own digital habits and make positive changes.

SHARE YOUR JOURNEY: Openly share your experiences, challenges, and successes with others. Your story can provide valuable insights and motivation for those looking to reduce their screen time and embrace a more balanced life.

BUILD A SUPPORTIVE COMMUNITY: Create or join communities focused on digital minimalism and mindful technology use. These communities provide mutual support, accountability, and encouragement, helping everyone stay committed to their goals.

CELEBRATE COLLECTIVE ACHIEVEMENTS:Acknowledge and celebrate the achievements of your community members. Collective celebrations foster a positive and motivating atmosphere, reinforcing the importance of balance and mindfulness.

A Final Word

Embracing a balanced life in today's digital world is a powerful and transformative choice. By taking the steps outlined in this book, you are prioritizing your well-being, strengthening your relationships, and enriching your overall life experience. Remember, the goal is not to eliminate technology but to integrate it in a way that supports and enhances your life.

As you move forward, continue to practice mindful technology use, engage in meaningful offline activities, and inspire others with your journey. Embrace the joy, clarity, and fulfillment that come from living a balanced life. Thank you for embarking on this journey with me, and here's to a future filled with intentional, enriching, and joyful experiences.

This conclusion ties together the main themes and strategies discussed throughout the book, emphasizing the importance of balance and mindfulness in a technology-driven world. It encourages readers to continue their journey toward a more fulfilling, balanced life and to inspire others to do the same.